RACING MANIA

MOTOCROSS

Bryan Stealey

This edition first published in 2010 in the United States of America
by Marshall Cavendish Benchmark.

Marshall Cavendish Benchmark
99 White Plains Road
Tarrytown, NY 10591
www.marshallcavendish.us

Library of Congress Cataloging-in-Publication Data
Stealey, Bryan.
Motorcross / by Bryan Stealey.
p. cm. — (Racing mania)
Summary: "Provides comprehensive information on the history, the famous faces, the design, and the
performance of the amazing machines behind motocross"—Provided by publisher.
Includes bibliographical references and index.
ISBN 978-0-7614-4386-5
1. Trail bikes—Juvenile literature. 2. Motocross—Juvenile literature.
I. Title.
TL441.S74 2010
796.7´56—dc22
2008055788

Cover: Q2AMedia Art Bank
Cover: Marcel Jancovic/Shutterstock; bg: Shutterstock
Half Title: Racer X
p4: Simon Cudby; p5: Simon Cudby; p6: Racer X; p7: Racer X; pp8-9: Simon Cudby; pp10-11: Simon
Cudby; p11(inset): Simon Cudby; pp12-13: Racer X; p12(inset): Simon Cudby; p14: Simon Cudby; p15:
Simon Cudby; p16: Simon Cudby; p17: Simon Cudby; pp18-19: Racer X; p19t: Simon Cudby; p20:
Racer X; p21: Racer X; p22: Racer X; p23: Racer X; p24: Racer X; p25: Racer X; p26: Racer X; p27br:
Simon Cudby; p27tl: Simon Cudby; p28: Simon Cudby; p29: Simon Cudby; p30: Simon Cudby; p31:
Simon Cudby; p32: Simon Cudby; p33: Simon Cudby; p34: Simon Cudby; p35: Simon Cudby; p36:
Simon Cudby; p37: Simon Cudby; p38: Matt Ware; p39: Matt Ware; p40: Racer X; p41: Racer X; p42:
Racer X; p43: Racer X; p44: Simon Cudby; p45: Simon Cudby; p45(inset): Press photo.

Created by Q2AMedia
Editor: Denise Pangia
Series Editor: Jim Buckley
Art Director: Sumit Charles
Client Service Manager: Santosh Vasudevan
Project Manager: Shekhar Kapur
Designer: Joita Das
Photo research: Shreya Sharma

Printed in Malaysia

1 3 5 6 4 2

CONTENTS

WHAT IS MOTOCROSS?

Motocross is one of the most exciting forms of racing in the world.

Many people consider motocross to be the original extreme sport. This popular form of racing involves motorcycles known as **dirt bikes** speeding around off-road courses. These narrow tracks usually include hills, jumps, tight turns, and other obstacles. Motocross races are run in both rain and sunshine. They usually involve close racing and lots of bumping. You might even see mind-blowing crashes! It is definitely not a sport for the timid.

At the beginning of a motocross race, two to forty riders line up behind a metal gate. The race starts when the gate drops. The competitors twist the **throttle** and roar into the first turn. This turn usually goes to the left. The first person to make it through the first turn—or the fastest through the starting line—has the **holeshot**. The start of a motocross race is one of the wildest moments in sports!

Few things in sports are as intense as the start of a motocross race.

Race winners get to stand on top of the podium.

Racers must finish a set number of laps. Most motocross tracks are close to 1 mile (1.6 kilometers) long—but it is a twisty mile! The rider who first crosses the finish line at the end of the race wins. A checkered flag waves to show the winner.

A single race is called a **moto**. Often, a motocross event includes two or three motos. Racers are awarded points for their finishes in each moto. The person with the most points wins the event. People of all ages and skill levels compete in the heart-pounding sport known as motocross.

■INSIDE STORY ||||||||

What Is Supercross?

Supercross is a lot like motocross, but there are some important differences. Motocross takes place on natural, outdoor courses. Supercross tracks are usually indoors and much smaller. Supercross tracks are filled with big jumps, very tight turns, and a series of bumps called whoops. **Amateur** riders enjoy racing motocross throughout the United States. Only professionals compete in Supercross races. The races are often held in major football and baseball stadiums. How popular is professional Supercross? NASCAR (National Association for Stock Car Auto Racing) is the only American motor sport that's bigger!

Motocross has been thrilling people all over the world for more than eighty years.

Motocross began outside of London, England, in 1924. Motorcycle riders started to hear about a new kind of event. It was being organized on a piece of land known as Camberley Heath. The race was called a *scramble*. Previous off-road events included trials sections. This is where participants would stop and perform tests or stunts on their bikes. But, in a scramble, the only thing that mattered was finishing first. Off-road racing was born.

Soon French riders became interested in this new form of sport. They are credited with renaming it *motocross*, which comes from the words *motorcycle* and *cross-country*. The rest of Europe soon caught on. Motorcycle manufacturers started to make specialized bikes that were fast on off-road courses. Racers mastered skills that allowed them to go over and through obstacles at amazing speeds. The sport's popularity grew. A professional series began in Europe.

The sport was introduced to the United States in the late 1950s. It grew slowly but steadily as riders experienced the thrill of this new form of racing. Yet, throughout the 1960s and early 1970s, the best European riders were still much faster than the top Americans.

Brad Lackey was one of the stars in the early days of motocross in the United States.

That began to change in the mid–1970s. That's when Americans like Gary Bailey, Jimmy Weinert, Jim Pomeroy, and Brad Lackey started to beat the Europeans. The Americans had finally arrived! Now racers from the United States are often at the front of the pack.

Motocross pioneer Jammin' Jimmy Weinert won three national championships in the 1970s.

■ INSIDE STORY ▐▌▐▌▐▌

Race What You Have

All modern-day racers compete on dirt bikes. That wasn't always the case. When scramble racing began, there were no such things as dirt bikes! Instead, racers would hop on their everyday motorcycles. They would ride them to the track, and then race them around the track! Today these motorcycles would seem as ancient as dinosaurs. Imagine what it might have felt like to go roaring down a steep hill without much safety equipment on these old bikes. It must have been crazy!

RUNNING THE SHOW

A motorcyclist group sets the rules in U.S. motocross.

The American Motorcyclist Association (AMA) is based in Pinkerington, Ohio. It is a group that helps motorcycle riders and racers. The AMA was formed in 1924, the year motocross was invented in Europe.

There are more than 1,200 AMA-based clubs throughout the United States. The group has more than 280,000 motorcyclist members. It's the largest motor sports organization in the world! Of course, many of these members aren't racers. They are people who just enjoy riding motorcycles.

When it comes to racing, the AMA is very important. The AMA sets rules for tracks in the United States. Because of these rules, when amateurs race in AMA events, they know the races will be well run and safe.

AMA Pro Racing runs professional motorcycle racing in the United States. In 2008 the AMA sold its Pro Racing division to the Daytona Motorsports Group. This is the same family that owns NASCAR. However, the races will still be considered AMA races.

The AMA Motocross Series and AMA Supercross Series are two of the most famous racing series. Motocross racers from all over the world come to the United States to compete in both of them. The best racers on these tours earn millions of dollars a year.

AMA officials make sure every bike is within the rules before it can be entered into a pro race.

The Hall of Fame

The AMA's Motorcycle Hall of Fame Museum is located in a building right next door to the AMA. It's filled with amazing things. For starters, it honors the most important people in the history of motorcycling. Many of the great motocross racers of all time are included in the Hall of Fame. Other motocross-related exhibits are also featured in the museum.

THE 450 CLASS

In professional motocross, the top racers ride 450 cubic-centimeter dirt bikes to fame and glory.

There are motocross bikes of all shapes and sizes, for every skill level. The smallest have 50 **cubic-centimeter** (cc) engines. These are raced by children as young as four years old! The best professionals race bikes with 450 cc engines.

The top pros in U.S. racing compete on dirt bikes with 450 cc four-stroke engines.

The top division of American professional motocross racing is called the 450 class. It includes only 450 cc bikes. Most racers compete on Japanese motorcycles built by Honda, Kawasaki, Suzuki, or Yamaha. Winning an AMA 450 Motocross Championship is the ultimate goal of most racers. Most racers begin in the smaller 250 class and then move up to larger bikes. The 250 cc engines in these smaller motorcycles give them slightly less power and speed.

To win the AMA 450 Motocross Championship, a racer must finish the season with the most points. Racers gain points based on their finishes throughout the season. The key is doing well week after week. One bad race can ruin a season!

Premier-class engines have 450 cc of volume, making them the biggest engines in U.S. professional racing.

■ INSIDE STORY ||||||

Different Strokes

Modern professional motocross bikes have **four-stroke engines**. Engines work when a long, round **piston** moves up and down in a narrow tube called a **cylinder**. In a four-stroke, the piston moves through the cylinder four times, repeatedly. When motocross first came to the United States, most racers used two-stroke engines. Today, all professional motocross racers compete on four-strokes.

THE 250 CLASS

Professional motocross racers usually start out in the 250 class.

Motocross racers start very young. A racer who is sixteen years old can get a professional license! Each year a new batch of teenagers joins the AMA Motocross Championship. If they were to start in the 450 class, they would immediately be racing against the best riders in the world. Instead, most choose to start their careers in the 250 class.

A 250 cc engine is much smaller than its 450 cc counterpart, but it's still very fast.

The Name Game

The main divisions of professional motocross racing have had many names. Early on, the most common engine sizes were 250 cc and 500 cc. Eventually, 125 cc bikes became more common and 500 cc bikes less so, and again the classes changed. In Europe there are three major divisions of professional racing—MX1, MX2, and MX3 classes. As recently as 2008 the classes in the United States were called the Motocross class and the Motocross Lites class. With all of these names, motocross can be confusing!

Of course, that doesn't mean that the 250-class racers are slow. In fact, the very fastest in the class can often beat the majority of the racers in the 450 class. In general, though, the 250 class is a good opportunity for pros to get their feet wet before racing the big engines.

One area in which motocross is different from Supercross is in the 250 class. In Supercross, the 250 class is broken down into two divisions. These are the Western Region and the Eastern Region. Each season, one champion is crowned from each region. There are two divisions in Supercross because so many 250-class racers are high school students. It is hard for the young riders to travel all over the country while in school. Motocross has just one 250 division. That division goes to every stop on the tour. It includes every 250-class racer. A 250 title in motocross is considered a major championship.

SAFETY FIRST

Motocross can be a dangerous sport, so it's important to be as safe as possible.

Before a motocross racer heads to the starting line, he or she has to put on safety gear. Every racer does his or her best to keep the bike on two wheels. Yet, everyone crashes from time to time. It's important to be as prepared as possible for these **wipeouts**.

- The helmet is the most important piece of safety gear. Helmets are made from lightweight, futuristic materials. They need to fit snugly and be strapped on correctly. Wearing a helmet greatly reduces injuries. All riders must wear one.

Goggles

Helmet

Gloves

Chest protector

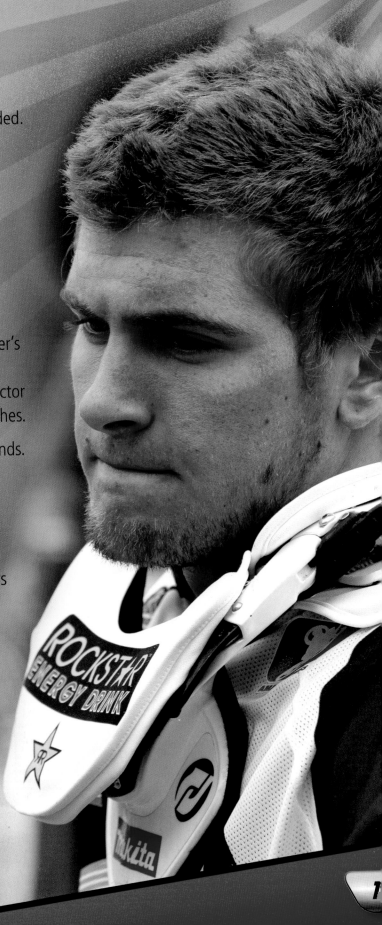

- Goggles cover a rider's eyes. They protect eyes from flying rocks and dirt.

- A rider's jersey and pants are lightly padded. They're also flexible and lightweight. This design allows air to flow through them easily. Motocross is a very demanding sport. A rider needs to be comfortable. This gives the rider a better chance of staying on the bike.

- A chest protector is a shell made of hard plastic that covers a rider's chest, shoulders, and back. It's worn over a rider's jersey. The chest pad makes a rider look like a modern **gladiator**. A chest protector deflects flying rocks. It also helps in crashes.

- Motocross racing is very hard on the hands. Drivers wear gloves for protection from debris. Gloves also keep their hands from getting blisters.

- Most racers also wear neck and knee braces made of plastic and metal. Riders who plan to compete with an injured wrist often wear a wrist brace.

- The boots are also very important. They give riders much-needed ankle support for going over tough terrain. They also protect them from burns in case their legs or feet touch hot engine parts.

Neck braces like this one worn by Ryan Dungey are common in the sport.

MOTOCROSS TRACKS

Racing outdoors always has its challenges. That's what makes it fun.

Motocross courses come in all shapes and sizes. They contain many different kinds of obstacles. The layout of a track depends mostly on the land upon which it is built. A track in a flat state like Kansas, for example, probably wouldn't have many hills in it. And a track in Pennsylvania wouldn't have many flat spots in it!

The layout of a motocross track is mostly determined by the land on which it is built.

This model shows the big elevation changes on a typical motocross track.

A motocross track usually starts with a long, straight piece of track that leads into the first turn. After that turn, riders begin to tackle the obstacles. Dirt bikes are made to jump. Motocross courses always have different kinds of jumps. There are single, double, and triple jumps. Riders clear one, two, and three mounds of dirt at a time. Other jumps have names such as tabletops, ski jumps, and step-ups. For many riders and fans, the jumps are the most exciting obstacles on the track.

Many tracks also have whoops. These are a series of small bumps lined up one after the other. Whoops are very much like **moguls** in snow skiing. Some riders take their time going through the whoops, which can be very challenging. Professionals often ride so quickly through them that they just skim across the tops of the bumps.

Outdoor tracks also have plenty of turns. The turns might snake through woods or up and down hills. Let's not forget the dirt. Some tracks have soft, mushy soil. Others are made of hard, rocky dirt. If it rains the track is called a *mudder*, thanks to the squishy mud caused by the rain. Motocross races happen rain or shine!

■ INSIDE STORY ‖‖‖‖‖

Earth Movers

Motocross track builders use a lot of dirt to shape jumps and turns. Special equipment makes their job easier. Tractors, bulldozers, and graders help to build tracks. The machines also help keep the tracks in racing shape. When hundreds of dirt bikes speed around a track, it gets chewed-up and rough. Track owners often use tractors to make the dirt smoother in between races.

SUPERCROSS TRACKS

Taking motocross indoors means making some big changes to the track.

Motocross tracks are all outdoors. Supercross tracks are usually in stadiums, which are much smaller. That means builders don't have much room to work with. Supercross tracks have many of the same obstacles that are used on motocross tracks. But in Supercross, these obstacles are usually much closer together. Supercross tracks almost never include hills.

The straight starting section of a Supercross track is flat. Once racers make it through the first turn, they face a constant stream of jumps until the lap is finished. Motocross tracks present plenty of opportunities for riders to get to full speed. Supercross tracks are tight and full of jumps. The goal is steady riding at high speeds. Racers who learn how to time the jumps have the fastest lap times and the best chance of winning.

Because Supercross tracks are almost always in stadiums, they're smaller and full of jumps.

Arena Supercross racing is only for professionals. These tracks are difficult. Jumps are usually very steep. Racers have to concentrate to make sure they're always ready for the next obstacle. Getting around the track quickly is hard enough. Imagine trying to do it side by side with other racers! The competition can be fierce. One little mistake can result in a painful crash—not to mention a bad finish.

Supercross races are held in major stadiums in big cities. Tens of thousands of people come out to watch. These races include laser shows, loud music, and fireworks. It's an exciting form of motocross racing that you have to see to believe.

Supercross track builders can fit many obstacles and turns into small spaces.

■INSIDE STORY ||||||

In the Pits

Fans who go to professional races often buy pit passes. These passes allow people to get into the pits, which is the area of the track where the race teams' mechanics work on the motorcycles. Fans have a chance to see their favorite racers and motorcycles up close. They can also get photographs with professional racers and collect autographs. Many industry companies also set up booths in the pits. They talk with fans about their products. Booths usually have gifts, like stickers and key chains, which fans can collect.

MOTOCROSS HEROES

Motocross has a rich, exciting history filled with legendary racers.

As long as there has been motocross, there have been motocross stars. Some racers have a combination of guts, brains, and ability that sends them to the top. The best of the best are loved by fans and feared by rivals.

Steve Stackable was an early champion of U.S. motocross.

Europeans were the greatest motocross racers in the early years of motocross. At first, English racers dominated. Jeff Smith, Dave Bickers, and Fred Rist were the fastest in the first years of international racing. This was during the late 1940s and 1950s, when most racers also rode English motorcycles. As the sport grew, other countries started to produce famous motocross stars. World champions have come from Belgium, Holland, Germany, Russia, and many other nations.

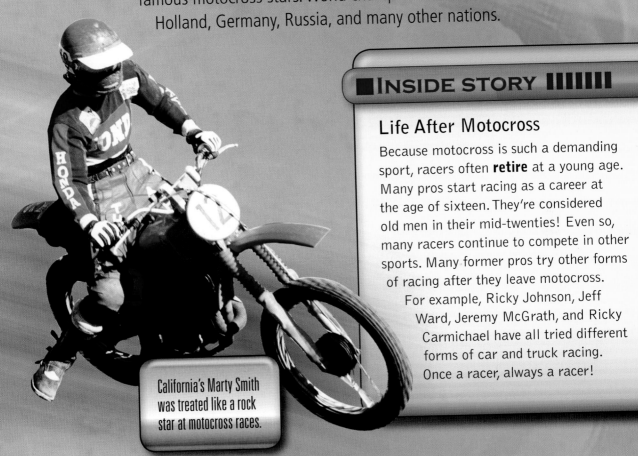

California's Marty Smith was treated like a rock star at motocross races.

▓ INSIDE STORY ▐▐▐▐▐▐

Life After Motocross

Because motocross is such a demanding sport, racers often **retire** at a young age. Many pros start racing as a career at the age of sixteen. They're considered old men in their mid-twenties! Even so, many racers continue to compete in other sports. Many former pros try other forms of racing after they leave motocross. For example, Ricky Johnson, Jeff Ward, Jeremy McGrath, and Ricky Carmichael have all tried different forms of car and truck racing. Once a racer, always a racer!

U.S. motocross stars were soon to follow. Racers such as Marty Smith, Barry Higgins, Steve Stackable, and Gary Bailey were among the first to challenge the Europeans. They paved the way for U.S. racers to become the best in the world.

Becoming a motocross hero is very difficult. It requires constant practice and exercise. Sometimes, even that isn't enough. Most motocross champions are born with a determination to work harder than other riders. Some top pros seem to have a natural ability on a motorcycle. It's as though they were born to ride.

THE MAN AND THE HURRICANE

Bob Hannah and Roger DeCoster were two of the most important racers in U.S. motocross history.

Bob "Hurricane" Hannah is considered the first real U.S. motocross superstar. He won seven AMA championships and dozens of races. Hannah started riding dirt bikes in the California desert at the age of seven. He started racing in 1974. Soon, Hannah was the most feared racer in the United States. Not only did he win more than everyone else, he also had more fans than anyone else. One of the reasons Hannah was so good was because of how hard he trained. When he wasn't racing, he was working out or riding in the desert. His determination helped him become one of the best racers ever.

Bob "Hurricane" Hannah was the first pro to take training very seriously.

■ INSIDE STORY ||||||

Flying High Again

While Roger DeCoster decided to stay in the sport after he quit racing, Bob Hannah did not. Instead, the "Hurricane" wanted to try another activity he was interested in: flying. Soon Hannah was racing again. This time it was in airplanes! These days, he owns a company called Hannah Aviation, in Idaho. His company sells airplanes of all kinds, from antiques to fancy jets. Yet, he's still treated like a motocross hero when he visits a race.

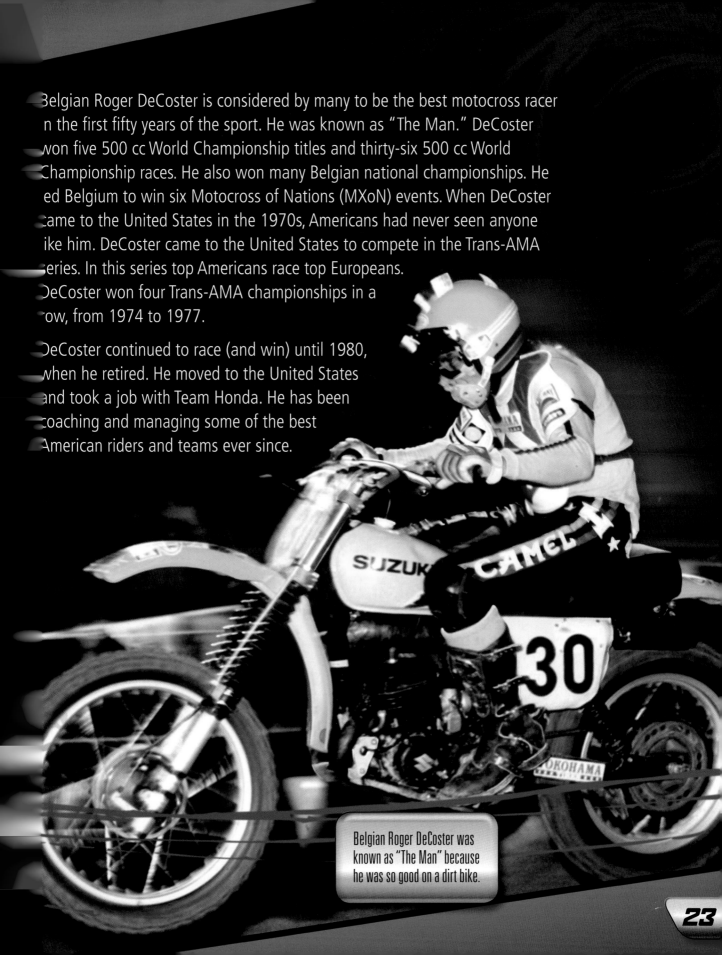

Belgian Roger DeCoster is considered by many to be the best motocross racer in the first fifty years of the sport. He was known as "The Man." DeCoster won five 500 cc World Championship titles and thirty-six 500 cc World Championship races. He also won many Belgian national championships. He led Belgium to win six Motocross of Nations (MXoN) events. When DeCoster came to the United States in the 1970s, Americans had never seen anyone like him. DeCoster came to the United States to compete in the Trans-AMA series. In this series top Americans race top Europeans. DeCoster won four Trans-AMA championships in a row, from 1974 to 1977.

DeCoster continued to race (and win) until 1980, when he retired. He moved to the United States and took a job with Team Honda. He has been coaching and managing some of the best American riders and teams ever since.

Belgian Roger DeCoster was known as "The Man" because he was so good on a dirt bike.

BAILEY VS. JOHNSON

Rivals David Bailey and Ricky Johnson battled hard to become the best of the 1980s.

David Bailey had a style on a dirt bike that people still talk about today.

David Bailey is one of the most loved motocross stars of all time. The California-born racer started slower than many other top pros, but he had one big advantage. Bailey's stepfather, Gary Bailey, had been a top professional motocross racer in the 1970s. Gary was also a well-known motocross teacher. David was a very willing student, and he turned pro by 1979.

Bailey had some success in 1980 and 1981. The mighty Team Honda noticed, and they hired him in 1982. On better motorcycles, Bailey's finishes improved. That year he finished near the top six times in motocross and Supercross. A year later, Bailey finally started to win races. In fact, he won the first Supercross race of the year, in Anaheim, California. Bailey was so fast that he won the championships in both Supercross and motocross. He had finally become a star! He would continue his winning ways until a crash during practice ended his career.

Bailey's biggest rival was another Californian named Ricky (R. J.) Johnson. R. J. turned pro soon after his sixteenth birthday. In 1981, his first full season, he was named the AMA Motocross Rookie of the Year. He won his first professional motocross championship in 1984. By the time R. J.'s career was over, in 1991, he had become one of the most successful racers in American history. He won seven championships, sixty-one races, and the hearts of thousands of fans.

▮INSIDE STORY ▮▮▮▮▮▮

Best Race Ever?

Many motocross racers consider the 1986 Anaheim Supercross race to be the best in the history of the sport. David Bailey and Ricky Johnson were Honda teammates that year, but they wanted to beat each other badly. That race, in front of a sold-out crowd, was unbelievable. Bailey and Johnson passed each other dozens of times throughout the night. The fans went crazy! When it was finally over, Bailey came out on top. People talk about the race to this day.

Ricky Johnson was as flashy on the track as he was fast.

WELCOME TO THE BIG TIME

Riders like Jeremy McGrath and Travis Pastrana helped introduce motocross to new fans.

The 1990s were all about Jeremy McGrath. The California-born rider was called "Showtime" by his fans. He became the most popular racer in the history of the sport. He was fast on any motorcycle, but he was an expert at Supercross. By the time his career was over, McGrath had won seventy-two Supercross races. That record will probably never be broken. He was also a seven-time AMA champion.

McGrath was a **BMX** racer until he was fourteen years old. BMX is like motocross, but riders use bicycles on shorter tracks. McGrath learned a lot on bikes, so he got a great start in motorcycles. Soon he was winning professional races. He became so good at Supercross that he rarely lost a race. He also made many fans by performing exciting tricks over the finish-line jump.

Jeremy McGrath was the first racer to become famous outside of motocross. He was in television commercials and on talk shows. He was a model for action figures and was in popular video games. No wonder fans called him Showtime!

Travis Pastrana is world famous for having the guts to do just about any stunt.

Another rider who helped introduce motocross to new fans was Travis Pastrana. This smiling kid from Maryland was a very fast amateur racer. He also became a pro champion. Pastrana's biggest problem was that he often got hurt. Staying healthy enough to win championships became difficult for him. He soon started to spend more time doing freestyle motocross events like the X Games. The gutsy daredevil was unstoppable at the new sport. While he often got hurt, Pastrana always managed to come back to give fans more excitement.

Jeremy "Showtime" McGrath performs his signature nac-nac trick.

Pastrana was the first rider to double-backflip a motorcycle.

▌INSIDE STORY ▐▐▐▐▐▐▐

The Nac-Nac

Jeremy McGrath helped to invent the sport of freestyle motocross racing. And he helped make it more exciting! When McGrath started to win races, he also started showing off in front of fans. He would usually perform a trick called a nac-nac after winning a race. To do this trick, McGrath would lift one foot off the foot peg. He'd swing the foot around the back fender so both of his legs were on the same side of the bike. The trick is considered tame now. Back then, it was unbelievable.

THE GOAT AND THE KING

Ricky Carmichael and Stefan Everts may be the two best motocross racers of all time.

Florida's Ricky Carmichael started riding on his family's three-wheeled motor bike at the age of three. Most kids can't even ride bicycles at that age! Carmichael loved being on a motorcycle. By the time he turned five years old, he was ready to race. It didn't take long for Carmichael to win major amateur events. By the time he was ready to turn pro at sixteen years old, he was the most successful amateur racer of all time.

Carmichael continued his winning ways as a pro racer. He was named the AMA Rookie of the Year in 1996. The next year he won his first professional motocross championship. Even though he was a winner, many fans thought he was too confident. He often heard more boos than cheers. Soon Carmichael won the fans over, and he just kept winning.

Ricky Carmichael is widely considered the GOAT of motocross: the Greatest of All Time.

"The King" of European motocross is definitely Stefan Everts, who won more races there than anybody else.

By the time his career was over in 2007, Carmichael had won a record 150 professional races, including motocross and Supercross. He also holds the record for most pro championships. That's why people call him the GOAT: the Greatest of All Time.

Carmichael was America's best. Belgium's Stefan ("The King") Everts was Europe's best. Everts retired from competition in 2006 with 101 world championship wins and 10 world championships.

Everts was born to ride. His father, Harry, was a four-time world champion. Young Everts rode a motorcycle with grace and style. He made it look easy. Everts was so good that he won races in the 125 cc, 250 cc, and 500 cc classes on one day in 2003. That achievement had never been accomplished before, and it hasn't happened since.

■ INSIDE STORY ⅠⅠⅠⅠⅠⅠ

Who's the Greatest?

An argument that often comes up between motocross fans is this: Who's better, Carmichael (left) or Everts? They raced each other so rarely that it's hard to say. Many fans of European motocross would pick Everts, while U.S. fans would usually choose Carmichael. They raced each other twice on the same size motorcycles. Carmichael won easily both times. That's enough proof for many who consider him to be the Greatest of All Time.

BREAKING BARRIERS

James Stewart and Ashley Fiolek have overcome many obstacles—on and off the track—to become motocross champions.

James Stewart is well on his way to becoming the next legendary racer. The 2008 AMA Motocross and Supercross Champion is the first African-American champion in the sport. This has led many people to compare him to golf's Tiger Woods.

Stewart has always been extremely fast. By the time he turned pro, he had broken Ricky Carmichael's record for amateur championships. As a young pro he won more Lites championships—250—than anyone in history. Now he wins on full-size bikes. There doesn't appear to be anyone in the world who can ride at his level. He even discovered a new way of jumping. It's called *scrubbing*, which means keeping jumps lower so that the wheels get more time on the dirt. Many riders now try scrubbing to go faster.

Even when James Stewart was an amateur, everyone knew he'd change motocross forever.

Stewart helped break down racial barriers in motocross. Women's motocross champion Ashley Fiolek is doing the same thing for racers with disabilities. Ashley has been deaf since birth. Her disability hasn't stopped her from becoming one of the fastest female motocross racers in the world.

Ashley won her first Women's Motocross Association (WMA) championship in 2008 at the age of seventeen! Ashley is living proof that everybody can achieve their dreams, no matter what obstacles stand in their way.

Ashley Fiolek doesn't let her disability keep her from pursuing her dreams of motocross greatness.

■ INSIDE STORY ||||||

Still Rolling

Ricky James was another rider who overcame obstacles. James was partly paralyzed in a terrible motocross crash. Amazingly, he was able to work his way back onto a specially modified dirt bike so he could ride again. He's even able to hit big jumps! The thrill of riding again set something off in James. He moved on to take part in Ironman triathlons. James won't let anything get in his way!

THE OLYMPICS OF MOTOCROSS

Motocross isn't usually a team sport, but it is at the Motocross of Nations.

Many people feel that the most important motocross race is the Motocross of Nations (MXoN). The race is held every year in a different place. Countries from all over the world send their three fastest riders. Three motos are held, and each team member gets to race in two of them. Riders score points based on their finishes. The team with the most points wins the prize. It is called the Peter Chamberlain Trophy.

Fans at the MXoN often dress in their country's colors and go wild with excitement.

Team USA has grown accustomed to winning the prestigious MXoN.

The first race had few spectators, and only three countries sent teams: Great Britain, Belgium, and Holland. That year, the British had the best scores, beating the Dutch and Belgium teams. More than 30,000 fans showed up. The MXoN quickly grew. It's still one of the biggest motocross events of the year.

Fans like the MXoN because it gives them a chance to see the best American-based racers compete against the best European-based racers. The MXoN is the only race of the year where the best from the two major motocross areas battle on the same track.

The most successful team in the history of the event is the United States, with eighteen victories. Great Britain is second with sixteen. Belgium is third with fourteen.

▌INSIDE STORY ▐▐▐▐▐▐

The Streak

The United States's eighteen wins in the MXoN are impressive. Even more amazing is that thirteen of them came in a row. Team USA didn't win the Peter Chamberlain Trophy until 1981. Then they didn't let go of it! They won every single MXoN from 1981 to 1993. It was the longest winning streak in the history of the event. Great Britain finally managed to stop the mighty Team USA by winning in 1994.

WOMEN'S MOTOCROSS

Men aren't the only motocross stars; just ask women racers.

Women have been racing motocross in the United States for decades, but it hasn't always come easy. Kerry Kleid would agree. The New Yorker decided in the early 1970s that she wanted to try to race against men. She signed up for a professional license and prepared for her first pro race. Yet, when she showed up at the track, AMA officials told her she wasn't allowed to race because she was a woman. Kleid didn't think that was fair. She threatened to take the AMA to court. The AMA changed its mind and allowed Kerry to race against the pros.

Tarah Gieger is one of the top female motocross racers in the world.

A professional women's race is just as intense as a men's race . . . and sometimes more so.

Women have been racing professionally ever since. The first organized series for women was called the Powder Puff National Championship. More than three hundred women racers roared around in front of thousands of fans. The next year the name was changed to the Women's Motocross Nationals.

Women's motocross has continued to grow. The current pro series, run by the Women's Motocross Association (WMA), takes place at the same time as the AMA Motocross Championship tour. WMA racers such as two-time champ Tarah Gieger, use the same tracks as the men, and race on similar motorcycles. The series attracts the top female racers in the world. Since 2008 there has also been a women's racing class held at the popular X Games.

■ INSIDE STORY ▐▐▐▐▐▐

Shooting Stars

Women's motocross features plenty of superstar racers. Ashley Fiolek is the new kid on the block. The best women's racer of all time is Jessica Patterson. She won five WMA championships. Tarah Gieger and Sarah Whitmore each have two championships, not to mention lots of sponsors and fans. Other top riders include Steffi Laier, Stefy Bau, and Tania Satchwell. Every year, their sport grows stronger.

THE SOUL OF THE SPORT

Making it to Loretta Lynn's for the Amateur Championships is the high point of every top amateur racer's season.

The pros are exciting to watch. Yet, the amateurs make motocross go 'round.

Every Sunday, on tracks throughout the world, racers put on their gear and push their motorcycles to the starting line. They climb aboard their bikes and fire them up. Their stomachs are full of butterflies as they await the dropping of the gate. When it falls, they take off as quickly as possible. They try to snag the holeshot and maybe even a trophy. Unlike professionals, these riders are not paid to be there. In fact, they usually pay for their own equipment and entry fees. These riders are amateurs. They are weekend warriors who are fast and slow, young and old. Racing doesn't make them rich. It just makes them happy.

Amateur motocross means big business. For every pro who has been paid to race, there are thousands of amateurs spending money to keep the industry going. With motorcycles, engine parts, travel, and fees, motocross is an expensive sport.

Of course, some young amateurs dream of turning pro someday. The fastest of these kids show their stuff in front of scouts at the world's biggest amateur motocross competition: the AMA Loretta Lynn's Amateur Championships. The weeklong event happens every August on the Tennessee ranch of country music legend Loretta Lynn. Riders are only invited to the event after winning two very competitive qualifying rounds. The most successful riders at Loretta Lynn's can land pro contracts before they're even sixteen years old. That's how stars Ricky Carmichael and James Stewart got their start.

Most riders will never make it to Loretta Lynn's, let alone turn pro. They simply race for the love of the sport.

Young amateurs need family support to reach the highest levels of motocross.

FOUR-WHEEL FUN

As any all-terrain vehicle (ATV) racer will tell you, motocross isn't just for dirt bikes.

When most people think of motocross, they think of dirt bikes flying around rugged tracks. Some racers have a different idea. They compete aboard four-wheel ATVs. These machines are bigger and heavier than dirt bikes, but they still move fast.

It is harder to pass in an ATV race because the machines are so large. The best racers seem to have eyes in the backs of their heads and are able to block approaching riders from passing them. This often results in very close racing that makes the fans go wild. This close action is one of the main reasons that ATV motocross is growing so rapidly.

Motocross racing on ATVs is growing in popularity as more fans discover the sport.

Because ATVs have four wheels instead of two, they move around the track very differently from dirt bikes.

ATV motocross racers compete on the same tracks as dirt bikers, often on the same day. They have their own professional organization. The top riders have good salaries and thousands of fans. But it hasn't always been so great for ATV motocross. For many years ATVs had a bad reputation. Many thought they were dangerous to ride. Some companies stopped making ATVs for racing. During much of the 1980s and 1990s, people had to fix up their own ATVs to make them race-ready. Soon, though, as many as seven companies began making ATV racers again. Today the sport is growing quickly. Fans hope it will become as popular as dirt bike motocross.

INSIDE STORY

The Grand Finale

Loretta Lynn's ranch is the site of the top ATV amateur event, called the ATV Dirt Days. Every year the last race of the professional ATV series is held on the same track on the country music legend's property. Hundreds of racers show up hoping to win. Thousands of fans come from all over the country to see the best ATV racers on the planet do battle on this famous track. It's as big as ATV motocross gets.

FLIPPING OUT

Freestyle motocross (FMX) is one of the craziest sports there is. That's why it's so popular.

FMX has nothing to do with racing. Instead, it's all about doing huge jumps and thrilling tricks to entertain fans. Many think the sport got its start from motorcycle distance jumpers like Evel Knievel. These daredevils would jump over cars, buses, and even shark tanks!

Freestyle motocross riders combine gymnastics and riding skills.

The idea of jumping for entertainment really took off, thanks to Jeremy McGrath. In the early to mid–1990s, McGrath thrilled Supercross fans by doing his signature nac-nac trick over the finish line. It helped make McGrath the most popular rider in the world.

In the 1990s race organizers decided that you didn't need a race to draw a crowd. FMX events became more common. They began in California. Soon FMX events were held throughout the world. Some professional motocross racers even stopped racing to focus on FMX. Many people thought the sport was a **fad** and wouldn't be around for long. They were very wrong! Instead, it gets bigger with each passing year.

Freestyle riders can safely learn difficult tricks by practicing them in a foam pit first.

The first tricks seemed crazy. FMXers did stunts like nac-nacs, heel-clickers, can-cans, and no-handers. In tricks like these, riders take their hands and feet off the bike in mid-air. Soon riders became more daring. Jumpers actually got off their bikes in mid-air and then got back on before landing. When riders started to do backflips, the sport changed forever.

Today, all top FMX riders perform backflips. Some have even managed double backflips. Riders are trying to learn front flips and barrel rolls, too! The way things have gone so far in this crazy sport, they'll probably succeed.

■ INSIDE STORY ||||||

The Foam Pit

How have freestyle riders gotten so good? They can thank foam pits. In the early days of FMX, making a mistake while practicing usually meant a violent crash. Riders started making foam pits. These pits are large wooden boxes filled with thousands of soft foam cubes. When riders are first learning challenging new tricks, instead of landing on dirt, they land in foam pits. These pits give riders more confidence. They can try maneuvers that are more difficult. Now, all top riders use foam pits to perfect their skills.

THE X GAMES

The X Games are the biggest showcase of action sports in the world.

When it comes to action sports, it doesn't get any bigger than the X Games. The Entertainment and Sports Programming Network's (ESPN's) annual events feature the best extreme athletes competing for gold, silver, and bronze medals. The first sports in X Games were skateboarding, surfing, and bicycling. Organizers added FMX. Soon, the Freestyle Moto X competition was the biggest of all the events.

Today, there are many FMX events at the X Games. For example, one high jump is called a Step-Up. It calls for riders to clear a high bar like a pole vault. There are also women's races and competitions for Best Trick. Motocross legends such as Jeremy McGrath, Ricky Carmichael, Chad Reed, Jeff Ward, Nate Adams, Mike Metzger, and Travis Pastrana have all been in the X Games.

Supermoto, which combines track racing and freestyle, is another X Games event. It is popular with motocross champions like Jeff Ward.

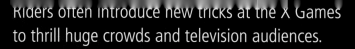

Riders often introduce new tricks at the X Games to thrill huge crowds and television audiences.

The Winter X Games also included a Moto X event for many years. The take-off and landing ramps were made of large mounds of snow. Athletes added spikes or studs to their tires to help them dig in. Problems started to arise when riders were faced with jumping in snowy conditions, as jumping in the snow was dangerous. Soon the promoters of X Games decided to keep the dirt bikes exclusively in the summer version.

Because riders like Ricky Carmichael have such excellent jumping skills, they often excel at X Games' Step-Up competition.

Motocross in the United States has come a long way, and it's just getting started.

What would you tell the first off-road racers about motocross today? You could tell them about all of the wonderful things that have happened, and they probably wouldn't believe you. The pioneers of the sport never could have guessed that one day motocross and Supercross would be so huge. They wouldn't believe that the sport packs stadiums and is popular on television.

The crowds at motocross races continue to grow as sports fans discover how exciting the events are.

The next question is, what's next? Will motocross ever be as big as car racing giants, Formula One and NASCAR? Will it grow to be as popular as the National Football League (NFL), Major League Baseball (MLB), or the National Basketball Association (NBA)? One thing is for sure: Motocross will continue to change and grow. More and more children are being introduced to it through television and the Internet. That can only mean good things for the sport.

In the future, motocross will see quieter motorcycles. Many even think that silent, electric engines could be the wave of the future. One way or the other, the technology behind the motorcycles will change with the times. Riders will get faster, jump higher, and earn even more money. Motocross racers should get ready. It's going to be one wild ride!

As long as manufacturers can keep the sound levels of dirt bikes down, the future of motocross is safe.

GLOSSARY

amateur	A person who takes part in a sport without being paid.
BMX	Bicycle motocross.
cubic centimeter	A measurement that is one centimeter wide, long, and high.
cylinder	One of several metal tubes inside a motorcycle engine.
dirt bike	A motorcycle with rugged tires and heavy springs made for riding on hilly dirt tracks.
fad	Something that is popular for only a short time.
four-stroke engines	An engine whose pistons go up and down four times each engine cycle.
gladiator	A type of ancient warrior who often wore metal or leather armor.
holeshot	The lead position on the first turn of a motocross race.
mogul	A humanmade bump on a ski run.
moto	One full race in motocross.
piston	The long, straight engine part that goes up and down in the cylinder.
retire	Stop taking part in a sport.
Supercross	Motocross held on stadium tracks.
throttle	The part of a motorcycle that sends gas to the engine to make it go.
wipeouts	Spectacular crashes.

FIND OUT MORE

BOOKS

Amick, Bill. *Motocross America*. Minneapolis, MN: MBI Publishing, 2005.
Travel the country with motocross fans and stars.

Casper, Steve. *Motocross Gallery*. Minneapolis, MN: MBI Publishing, 2006.
A photo-filled book about motocross bikes.

Perritano, John. *American MX: From Backwater to World Leader*.
St. Catherines, Ontario, Canada: Crabtree Publishers, 2008
A brief history of American motocross stars and races.

Poolos, J. *Travis Pastrana, Motocross Superstar*. New York:
Rosen Publishing, 2005.
An inside look at one of today's hottest freestyle MX stars.

WEBSITES

Visit these websites for more information.

www.espn.go.com/action
This action-packed site includes information on freestyle
motocross, the X Games, and motocross stars.

www.pbskids.org
If you search "motocross" on this site, you'll find a way
to use motocross skills to make a science project!

www.racerxonline.com
Packed with video and photos, this site covers the world
of pro motocross and Supercross inside and out.

INDEX